Python – A Nuts and Bolts Guide for

Copyright © 2018 by Russell I F Bryant. All Rights Reserved.

All rights reserved. No part of this book may be reproduced in any form or by any electronic or mechanical means including information storage and retrieval systems, without permission in writing from the author. The only exception is by a reviewer, who may quote short excerpts in a review.

Python and the Python Logo are trademarks or
registered trademarks of the Python Software Foundation.

Cover designed by Russell I F Bryant

Visit our website at www.edulito.com

Second Printing: December 2018

Edulito

ISBN: 9781792811777

CONTENTS

	ACKNOWLEDGMENTS	3
1	PYTHON BASICS	4
2	THE USE OF VARIABLES	8
3	THE USE OF DATA TYPES	12
4	THE USE OF STRING MANIPULATION	15
5	THE USE OF SEQUENCES AND SELECTION	25
6	THE USE OF ITERATION	34
7	THE USE OF LISTS (ARRAYS)	42
8	FILE HANDING OPERATIONS	54
9	USING FUNCTIONS AND PROCEDURES	58
10	CREATING A BOARD GAME	62
11	CREATING A DATABASE USING PYTHON LISTS	72

ACKNOWLEDGMENTS

I have to start by thanking my friends and family for always being supportive through the process of developing this book. I would like to thank my colleagues and the students at Walthamstow School for Girls for helping me test out and refine the activities and tasks in this book. I would also like to thank the Python community for their support.

1. Python Basics

The Characteristics of a Successful Programmer

Programming is basically problem solving. To be a successful programmer the most important requirement is to be someone who doesn't give up easily. No matter how stuck you get it's best just to stick with it and eventually you'll have one of those light bulb moments where it all suddenly makes sense.
It will be tempting when you get stuck to ask someone to help you, and there is nothing stopping you taking advantage of someone else's experience, but in the long run this will ultimately slow down your own progress.

Successful problem solving requires logical thinking and the ability to break down complicated problems into smaller, less complicated problems. Try your best to concentrate on the bits of the problem that are relevant and ignore the rest. The reality is that it's best to take an approach that suits the way you think. If you're the kind of person who needs to draw what you're thinking, then go ahead and make a drawing. If you're not that person, it doesn't matter, as long as you do whatever you need to do to understand and then solve the problem.

What is Python?

Python is a commonly used, high level programming language, that has been used to code apps, such as Instagram.
To learn how to code using Python you will need to install a Python IDE on to your computer e.g. Python IDLE.

An IDE (Integrated Development Environment) is a software tool that helps you to write, debug and test a program. Python IDLE is a simple, easy to use IDE. There are alternatives, but this guide uses Python IDLE.

When you first open Python IDLE you will see the **Interactive** window or **shell**. This interactive window is ideal for writing short, simple programs. You always write code in the interactive window after the chevrons (>>>).

It looks like this:

```
File  Edit  Shell  Debug  Options  Window  Help
Python 3.6.5 (v3.6.5:f59c0932b4, Mar 28 2018, 16:07:46) [MSC v.1900 32 bit (Inte
l)] on win32
Type "copyright", "credits" or "license()" for more information.
>>>
```

Writing your first Python program

Make sure that you have Python open and that you are using the interactive window.

Task 1.1

Type **print("Hello World")** into the interactive window.

The **print** statement is used to let the program know that you want to **display** whatever is inside the brackets. Python will read your program and display the output:

```
>>> print("Hello World")
Hello World
>>>
```

Activity 1.1

Now write a program that will display your name.

Getting Python to do calculations

Python can also be used to carry out calculations. Write each of the examples individually into Python and press enter on the keyboard. The symbols used are called **operators**.

Name	Symbol in Python	Example
Addition	+	2+2
Subtraction	-	5-2
Multiplication	*	3*3
Division	/	20/4
Remainder	%	20%6
Exponent (to the power of..)	**	2**3
Division (no remainder)	//	8//5

This is the output in Python:

```
>>> 2+2
4
>>> 5-2
3
>>> 3*3
9
>>> 20/4
5.0
>>> 20%6
2
>>> 2**3
8
```

When using Python, you need to know the order in which the calculations take place.
For this you must use **BODMAS**.

Brackets - Start with calculating anything inside the brackets (from left to right).

Order - Do anything involving a power or a square root next (from left to right).

Division/Multiplication -multiplication and division rank equally, so you go from left to right in the sum.

Addition/Subtraction-subtraction and addition rank equally, and so you go from left to right in the sum.

Activity 1.2	
Predict the output produced by each of these calculations and then enter each calculation into the Python interactive window. Were you correct?	**Python Output**
50/10+3	
(7-2)*8	
7**2+(1+7-8)	
8/2*8/8+(100-90)	

The importance of using the correct syntax

Like any language, including English, it is important that you are careful as you enter code into Python. You must use the correct syntax. If you make a mistake you will get a syntax error and the program will not work. As you develop your programming skills you must be careful to follow the rules/syntax used in Python.

For example, whenever you write text (in Python this is known as a **string**) you must always use speech marks, or you will get a syntax error.

```
>>> print(Hello World)
SyntaxError: invalid syntax
>>>
```

Activity 1.3
Look at the example calculations below. In each case what would be the output? Once you have completed the calculations enter them into the interactive window in Python to see whether you were correct. (a) 6*8/8*(4+2) (b) 2**2/(1**2) (c) 16+8+(9/3*17) (d) 22*18/(22+22-6**2)

2. The Use of Variables

What is a variable?

Variables are used in computer programs to store a piece of information. For example, if you create a computer program that asks for a person's name. A variable can be used to store the person's name. A variable is like a box that can only store one piece of information at a time.

Using the Editing Window

Our programs are now going to get a bit more complicated and so we are going to use the **editing** window. The editing window lets you create longer programs that won't do anything until you run them.

Open the Python Interactive (shell) window and then select **New** from the **File** menu.
This will open the editing window. When you use the editing window you must save the program before you can run it.

Task 2.1

Write this program using the editing window:

```
File  Edit  Format  Run  Options  Windows  Help
name=input("What is your name?: ")
print("Hi",name,", I'm pleased to meet you.")
```

This program uses a **variable** called **name**.

input is used to tell the computer that you are expecting the person using the program to enter something, and in this case, you are expecting them to enter a name.

Once the person has entered a name, the **variable** is **assigned** this value.

print is used to **output** information, which in this case is a mixture of text strings and the value assigned to the variable.

Now make sure you have saved the program and then run it (select **Run module** from the **Run** menu).

When you output the program, it will ask you to enter a name. Once you have entered a name using the keyboard and clicked enter, the sentence will be displayed.

```
>>>
What is your name?: Aisha
Hi Aisha , I'm pleased to meet you.
>>>
```

Activity 2.1

1. Write a program that asks a person their first name, their surname and the name of their favourite animal. The program then displays a sentence that welcomes them and says who they are and what their favourite animal is.

2. How many variables did you use in the program?

Constants

Sometimes the data item being stored will not change i.e. it will **not** be a variable. These items of data are called **constants**.

E.g. the program below uses Pi to calculate the circumference of a circle. Pi is a constant and will always be 3.14. The formula is circumference = 2 x pi x radius is used to calculate the circumference.

Task 2.2

Write this program using the editing window:

```
#Calculate the circumference of a circle using the constant Pi
pi=3.14
radius=2
print("The circumference is: ",2*pi*radius)
```

Here is the output when you run this program:

```
>>>
The circumference is:    12.56
```

Activity 2.2

Write a program to calculate the area of a circle using the constant pi and the variables radius and area.

The formula is **area=pi*radius**2**

The program displays a message: The area is …..

Choosing an appropriate variable name

Python syntax requires that the variable name conforms to particular rules.
- There must be no spaces in the variable name e.g. it cannot be **first name**
- The variable name must not start with a number e.g. it cannot be **5first_name**

Tips for using appropriate variable names

- Use an underscore to link words e.g. **first_name**
- Use a name that makes sense e.g. don't use data1 for first name use **first_name**
- Name all variables in a consist way e.g. **first_name, telephone_number** etc
- Always start with a **letter**
- Remember that variable names are case sensitive **first_name** is not the same as **first_Name**
- Don't name variables using words that are reserved keywords in Python. You can type help("keywords") in the interactive window (shell) to get a list of reserved words.

List of reserved words

```
>>> help("keywords")

Here is a list of the Python keywords.  Enter any keyword to get more help.

False               def                 if                  raise
None                del                 import              return
True                elif                in                  try
and                 else                is                  while
as                  except              lambda              with
assert              finally             nonlocal            yield
break               for                 not
class               from                or
continue            global              pass
```

Activity 2.3

Using an example for each, explain the meaning of the following terms:

Variables, constants, operators, inputs, outputs and assignments

---

Assigning multiple values

You can assign more than one variable in a line of code. The code from the previous example has been rewritten so that there are only two lines of code.

Task 2.3

Write this program using the editing window:

```
pi,radius=3.14,2
print("The circumference is: ",2*pi*radius)
```

Activity 2.4

Which of these variable names will cause a syntax error if they are used in a Python program?

- Surname
- postcode
- 5x
- x5
- GreenflyNumbers
- uSERnAME
- global

3. Use of Data Types

Python will use **data types** to decide how to handle a particular type of data. Each variable will be one of **four** data types when using Python.

Data Type	Name in Python	When is it used
String	str	This is used for variables that store text. To identify a string in python you put the text inside speech marks (can be double speech marks or single speech marks). **E.g. "Hello World"**
Character	str	This is used for variables that store one single character. **E.g. "a"**
Integer	int	This is used for variables that store a positive or negative whole number. As it is only storing a whole number it uses up less memory than if it was to store a decimal number. **E.g. 32**
Real	float	This is used for variables that store a decimal number. When you use Python, you must use the word float for this data type. **E.g. 32.91819**
Boolean	bool	This is used when there are only two possible values. This could be **True** or **False**. E.g. this is used when a program needs to find out whether something is right or wrong.

Task 3.1

Write these two programs using the editing window. They are very similar but produce a different output. As you can see from these programs it is very important that you choose the correct data type or the program may not produce the outcome you would like.

Example 1   Example 2

```
x="2"
y="2"
print(x+y)
```

Example 1 uses a **string** data type.

```
x=2
y=2
print(x+y)
```

Example 2 uses an **integer** data type.

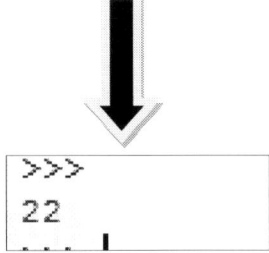

```
>>>
22
```

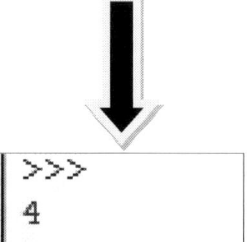

```
>>>
4
```

How to check the data type of a variable

You can find out the data type of a variable by using (type(x)) where the variable is called x.

Task 3.2

These three examples show how to find out the data type of a variable.
Write each of these three programs using the editing window and then after you run each program use **type(x)** and **type(y)** to find out the data types in each case.

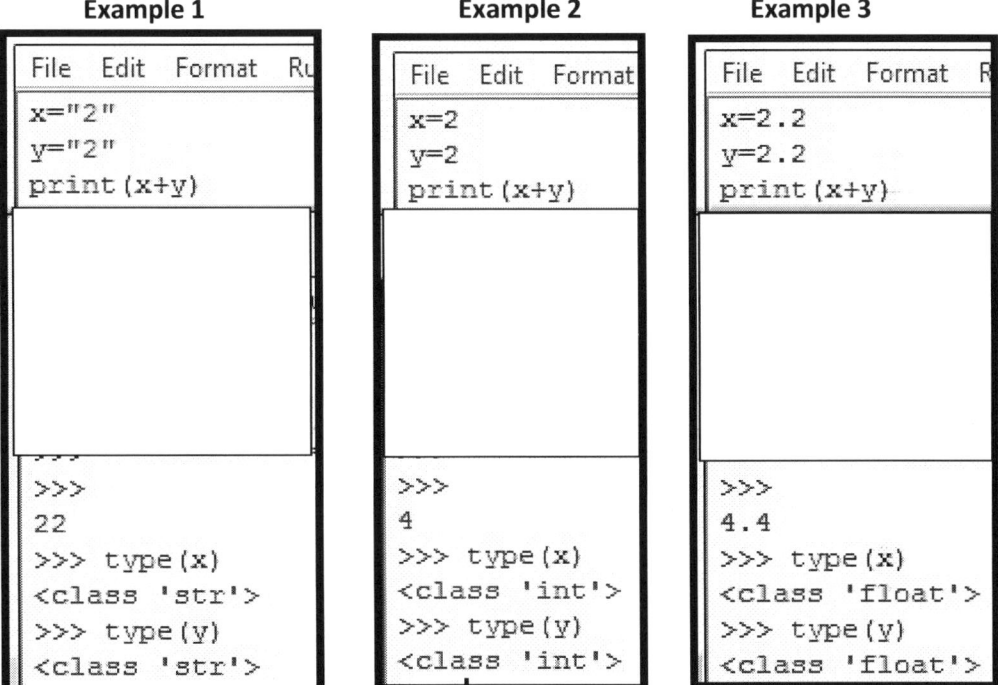

Casting

Sometimes when you write a program you need to be able to change a variable that has one data type to another data type. This is called **casting**.
In the example below both x and y start off with the data type **string**, but then they are **cast** into a different data type **integer**.

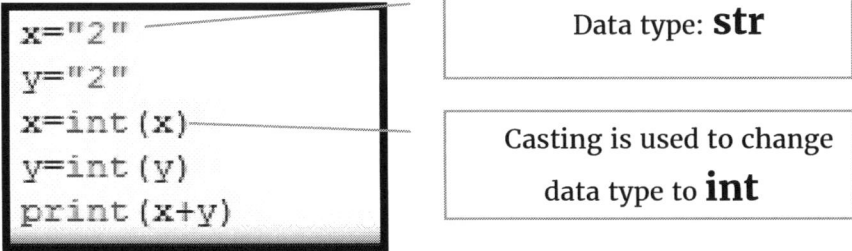

Activity 3.1

Write a program to calculate the **circumference** of a circle, using the constant **pi** and the variable **radius**.

Start by:
- assigning the value 3.14 to pi using the data type string (**str**)
- assigning the value 4 to radius using the data type string (**str**)

Then:
- use **casting** to change the data type for pi from string to **float** (Float is the data type used for decimal numbers)
- use casting to change the data type for radius from string to **integer** (Integer is the data type used for whole numbers)

The formula is **circumference=2*pi*radius**

The program displays a message: The circumference is:

4. The Use of String Manipulation

Should I use double quotation marks or single quotation marks?

Using double or single quotation marks generally produces the same output.

Task 4.1

Write this program using the interactive window (shell)

```
>>> print('Welcome to Python')
Welcome to Python
>>> print("Welcome to Python")
Welcome to Python
>>>
```

How do I display text over a number of lines?

You can use triple quote marks to display text over a number of lines.

Task 4.2

Write this program using the interactive window (shell)

```
>>> print("""
Welcome to the
world of programming
using Python""")

Welcome to the
world of programming
using Python
```

How do I use quote marks in a string?

You can use single quotation marks for this.

Task 4.3

Write this program using the interactive window (shell)

```
>>>
>>> print('Is this really "Python"?')
Is this really "Python"?
>>>
```

Using Escape Characters

Sometimes you need to perform an action inside the string. To do this you use **escape characters**.

When using single quotation marks, you can use \\ to show a backslash in your output.

Task 4.4

Write this program using the interactive window (shell)

```
>>> print('C:\\Drive')
C:\Drive
```

Task 4.5

When using single quote marks, you can use \' to show an apostrophe in your output.

Write this program using the interactive window (shell)

```
>>> print('It was Dave\'s program')
It was Dave's program
```

Task 4.6

When you want to display text on a new line in your program.

Write this program using the interactive window (shell)

```
>>> print("This is the first line\nThis is the second line")
This is the first line
This is the second line
```

Task 4.7

When you want to indent or tab your text.

Write this program using the interactive window (shell)

```
>>> print("Item 1\tItem 2\tItem 3")
Item 1   Item 2   Item 3
```

Handling strings in a program

When you write a program, you will often need to manipulate strings.

How do I find the length of a string?

Task 4.8

Use len(variable_name)

Write this program using the editing window.

```
sentence=input("Enter your sentence here: ")
print("The length of your sentence, including spaces is....",len(sentence))
```

Here is the output when you run this program:

```
Enter your sentence here: Welcome to earth
The length of your sentence, including spaces is.... 16
```

How do I change the string to UPPER case?

Task 4.9

Use variable_name.upper()

Write this program using the editing window.

```
sentence=input("Enter your sentence here: ")
print(sentence.upper())
```

Here is the output when you run this program:

```
>>>
Enter your sentence here: Welcome to Earth
WELCOME TO EARTH
```

How do I change the string to lower case?

Task 4.10

Use variable_name.lower()

Write this program using the editing window.

```
sentence=input("Enter your sentence here: ")
print(sentence.lower())
```

Here is the output when you run this program:

```
>>>
Enter your sentence here: Welcome to Earth
welcome to earth
>>>
```

How do I change the string to capitalise the first letter?

Task 4.11

Use variable_name.capitalize()

Write this program using the editing window.

```
sentence=input("Enter your sentence here: ")
print(sentence.capitalize())
```

Here is the output when you run this program:

```
Enter your sentence here: welcome to earth
Welcome to earth
>>>
```

How do I change the string to capitalise the first letter of each word?

Task 4.12

Use variable_name.title()

Write this program using the editing window.

```
sentence=input("Enter your sentence here: ")
print(sentence.title())
```

Here is the output when you run this program:

```
Enter your sentence here: welcome to earth
Welcome To Earth
>>>
```

How do I replace one letter with another letter in a string?

Task 4.13

Use variable_name.replace(x,y)

Write this program using the editing window.

```
sentence=input("Enter your sentence here: ")
print(sentence.replace("e","a"))
```

Here is the output when you run this program:

```
Enter your sentence here: Welcome to Earth
Walcoma to Earth
```

How do I return a sub-string of the original string?

Task 4.14

Use variable_name[x:y]

Write this program using the editing window.

```
sentence=input("Enter your sentence here: ")
print(sentence[0:7])
```

Here is the output when you run this program:

```
Enter your sentence here: Welcome to Earth
Welcome
```

String Alignment

You sometimes need to format your string. For example, you might want the text on the left, on the right or in the centre.

How do I make text appear on the left?
Task 4.15

Use <

Write this program using the editing window.

```
sentence=input("Enter your sentence: ")
print('{:<30}'.format(sentence))
```

Here is the output produced when you run this program:

```
Enter your sentence: Welcome to Earth
Welcome to Earth
```

How do I make text appear on the right?

Task 4.16

Use >

Write this program using the editing window.

```
sentence=input("Enter your sentence: ")
print('{:>30}'.format(sentence))
```

Here is the output when you run this program:

```
Enter your sentence: Welcome to Earth
              Welcome to Earth
```

How do I make text appear in the centre?

Task 4.17

Use ^

Write this program using the editing window.

```
sentence=input("Enter your sentence: ")
print('{:^30}'.format(sentence))
```

Here is the output when you run this program:

```
Enter your sentence: Welcome to Earth
        Welcome to Earth
```

How do I add asterisks around a centred title?

Task 4.18

Write this program using the editing window.

```
sentence=input("Enter your sentence: ")
print('{:*^30}'.format(sentence))
```

Here is the output when you run this program:

```
Enter your sentence: Welcome to Earth
*******Welcome to Earth*******
```

How do I use formatting to create a table of results?

You can simply print a set of data without using formatting, but it does not look very professional and is harder to read. Here is a table without formatting:

```
Car prices
Dacio Sandero 7395
Suzuki Celerio 7999
Skoda Citigo 8995
Peugeot 108 9349
```

Task 4.19

Write this program using the editing window.

```
c1="Dacio Sandero"
c2="Suzuki Celerio"
c3="Skoda Citigo"
c4="Peugeot 108"
p1=7395
p2=7999
p3=8995
p4=9349
print("Car prices")
print("{0:<15}{1:<4}".format("Car Type","Price"))
print("{0:<15}{1:<4}".format(c1,p1))
print("{0:<15}{1:<4}".format(c2,p2))
print("{0:<15}{1:<4}".format(c3,p3))
print("{0:<15}{1:<4}".format(c4,p4))
```

Here is the output when you run this program:

```
>>>
Car prices
Car Type       Price
Dacio Sandero  7395
Suzuki Celerio 7999
Skoda Citigo   8995
Peugeot 108    9349
```

Activity 4.1

the cow jumped over the moon

1. Using Python change the string above to display using:

    A. All words in upper case
    B. Capitalise the first word in the sentence
    C. Capitalise all words in the sentence

2. Create a table using Python to display the following results:

Pets - How long do they live?

Dogs 13 years Cats 15 years Gold Fish 8 years Hamster 3 years rabbit 7 years

5. The Use of Sequences and Selection

When creating a computer program there are a number of **structures** that can be used.

Sequences

Some programs are very straightforward. Each instruction follows the previous instruction until the program is complete. The program below is an example of a **sequence**. The first line of code is run, then the second line of code, followed by the third line of code.

```
name=input("What is your name?: ")
age=int(input("How old are you?: "))
print ("Hi",name,"I can't believe you are",age,"years old")
```

A flow chart can also be used to represent this **sequence**:

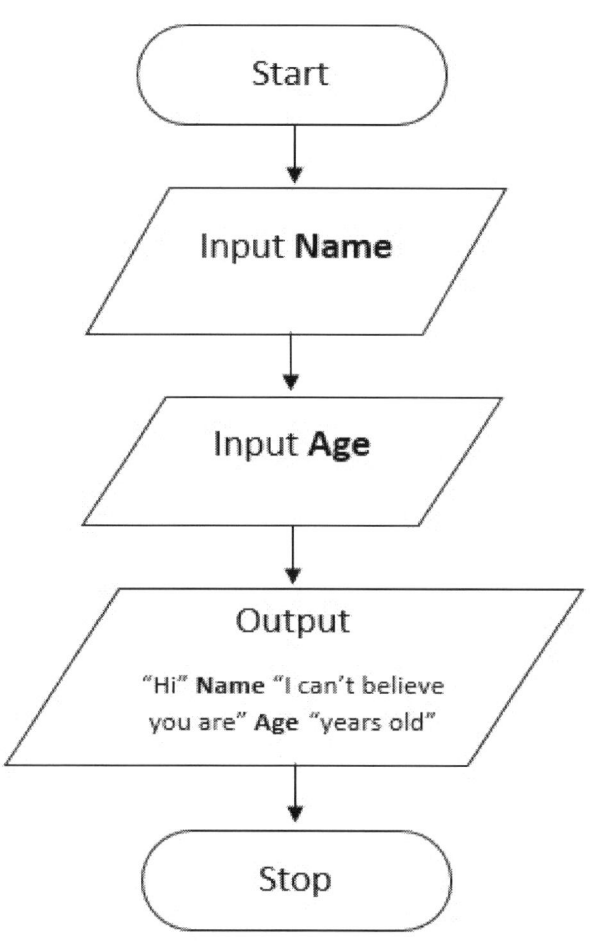

Comparison (Relational) Operators

These are often used in programming to compare two values and to determine whether one value is less than, greater than or equal to another value.

Here is a list of Comparison (Relational) Operators:

Operator	Meaning	Example
==	Are both values the same?	>>> 3==8 False
!=	Are the values not equal?	>>> 3!=8 True
<	Is the first value less than the second value?	>>> 3<8 True
>	Is the first value greater than the second value?	>>> 3>8 False
<=	Is the first value less than or equal to the second value?	>>> 3<=8 True
>=	Is the first value greater than or equal to the second value?	>>> 3>=8 False

Boolean (Logical) Operators

Operator	Meaning	Example

AND	Checks whether BOTH conditions are True or False. Therefore, BOTH conditions must be True for it be True.	`>>> x=10`
		`>>> x>9 and x<100`
		`True`

OR	Checks whether EITHER condition is True or False. Therefore, if EITHER condition is True it is True.	`>>> x=50`
		`>>> x<40 or x>10`
		`True`

NOT	This does the opposite of the existing value. True becomes False and False become True	`>>> x=30`
		`>>> y=10`
		`>>> not(x<y)`
		`True`

Activity 5.1

1. Write a program using a **sequence** that includes at least 4 lines of code that asks someone their name, their age and their favourite place to go on holiday. The program then displays the person's name, age and favourite holiday destination.

2. Using the **Python shell**, find out whether the following programs output true or false.
   a. 7==19
   b. 7!=19
   c. 7>19
   d. 7<19
   e. 19>=7
   f. 19<=7

3. Using the **Python shell**, find out whether the following programs output true or false. In all cases x=10 and y=20.

   a. x==y/2 and x>=9
   b. y/x==2 and y>=10
   c. x+y==20 or y+x==30
   d. x>=11 or y>=31
   e. not(x+y==30) and y==20
   f. not(x+y==30) or y==20

Selection

As mentioned at the beginning of this chapter, some algorithms/programs are very straightforward. Each instruction follows the instruction before until the program is complete. However, sometimes when you are writing an algorithm/program there needs to be a choice. E.g.

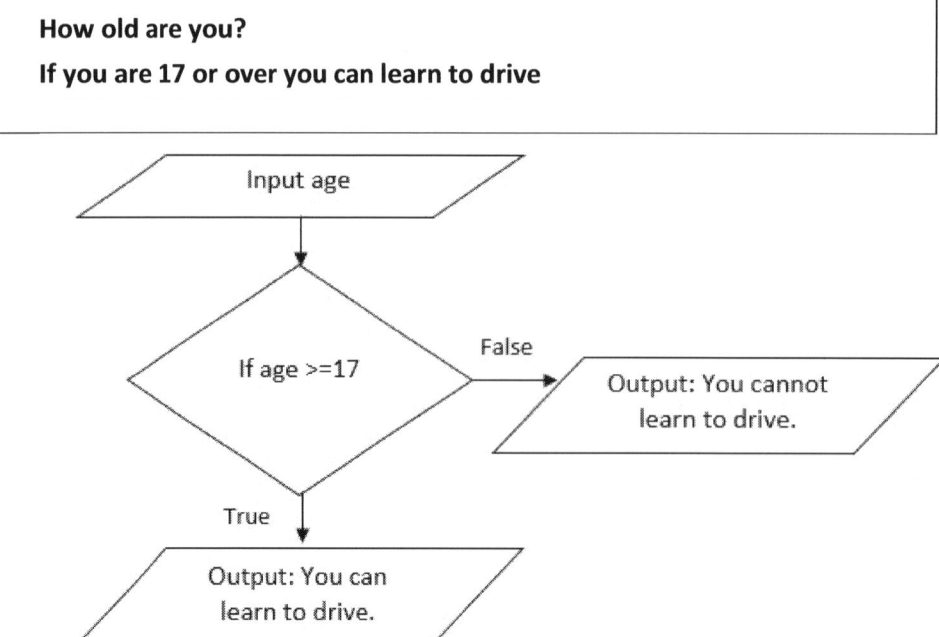

Indented code

Whenever you use selection the code must be indented to show that the action of selecting something is occurring "inside" the main program. After you type a colon Python Idle automatically indents the next line of code. All subsequent lines of code that are part of the selection must also be indented. When you complete Task 5.1 look out for the indentation.
E.g.
This is not indented.
    This is indented.

Simple IF statement

When you use **selection**, there is always a **test** or **condition**. In the example shown on page 28 the test is whether you are 17 or over. E.g. If the person who is being asked is 21 then the condition is **True**.

Task 5.1

Write this program using the editing window.

```
age=int(input("How old are you?: "))
if age >= 17:
    print("You can learn to drive")
```

Here is the output when you run this program:

```
How old are you?: 21
You can learn to drive
```

If then Else Statement

The above code shows a **simple if** that only deals with a condition that is **True**, but usually we need to deal with both possible outcomes from a test or condition. To do this we use **IF** then **ELSE**. In relation to the example shown above
- IF the person who is being asked is 17 or more then the condition is **True**.
- ELSE the condition is **False**.

In this example the statement displayed depends on whether the statement is **True** or **False**.

Task 5.2

Write this program using the editing window.

```
age=int(input("How old are you?: "))
if age >= 17:
    print("You can learn to drive")
else:
    print("You cannot learn to drive")
```

Here are the TWO possible outputs when you run this program. The output will change in relation to the age entered:

```
How old are you?: 21
You can learn to drive
>>>
```

```
How old are you?: 16
You cannot learn to drive
```

This **IF** then **ELSE** can also be represented using a flow chart.

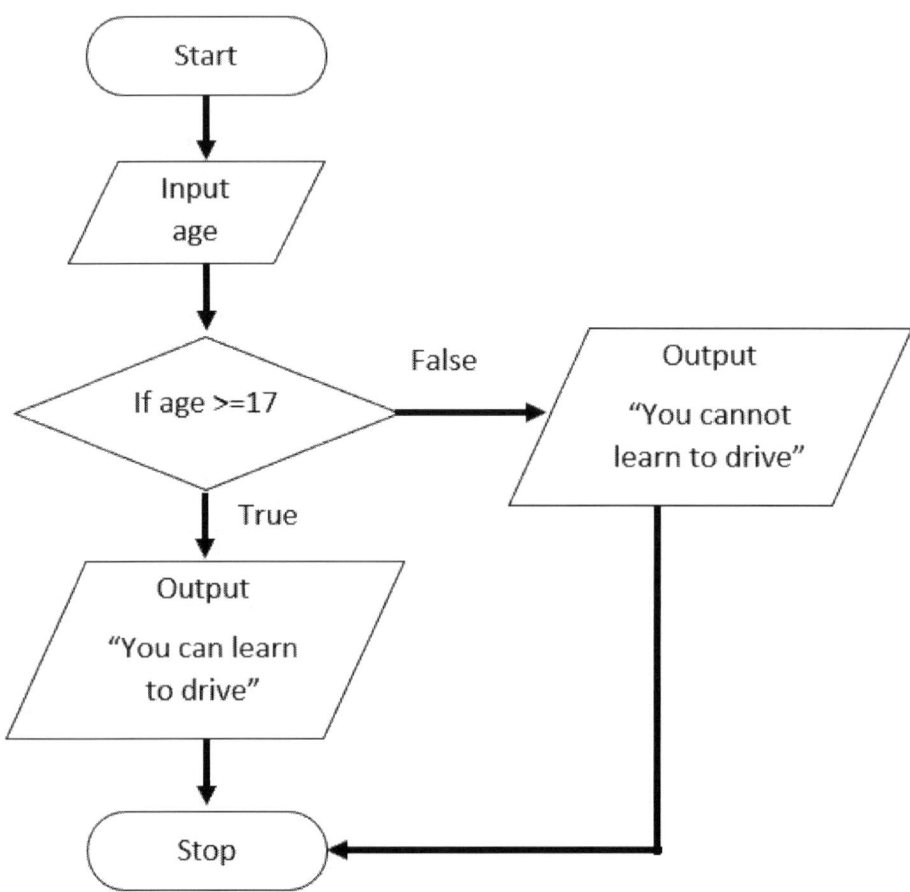

Activity 5.2

1. You work for passport control. You have been asked to write a program that sends out the correct form for passport renewal. If the person applying for the passport is under 16 they will need to be sent a "Child" application form. Anyone else applying must be sent the "Adult" application form.

2. You have been asked to write a program that manages security on the personal details stored on a database. Your program must store a particular person's username and their password. When this person tries to login, if their username and password are both entered correctly, they will be allowed to continue. However, if either one of these is entered incorrectly, they will not be able to proceed and they will receive a message telling them that either their password or username is incorrect.

3. You work for Twitter and you have been asked to create a program that informs the user if they have used too many characters in their message. The program allows you to enter your message and then the program calculates the length of the message in characters. If the message is greater than 140 characters, you get a warning message to say that your message is too long. (Hint: You will need to use **len(variable_name)**).

IF and ELIF Statements

If then Else can be used if there is one condition, but sometimes you have more than one condition and in this case, you will need to use IF and ELIF statements.
Here is the structure the code should follow.

```
if Condition 1= True:
    Do Code 1
elif  Condition 2= True:
    Do Code 2
else:
    Do Code 3
```

For example, if you have a number of test results you can use a program to generate a grade for each student.
This structure can be used for as many conditions as you want.

Task 5.3

Write this program using the editing window.

```python
test_mark=int(input("Enter test mark here: "))
if test_mark >=80:
    print("You have achieved Grade A")
elif test_mark >=60:
    print("You have achieved Grade B")
elif test_mark >=40:
    print("You have achieved Grade C")
else:
    print("You have Failed")
```

Here is the output when you run this program:

```
Enter test mark here: 62
You have achieved Grade B
```

Nested IF statements

Some programs have one if statement nested inside another if statement. For example:

Ruby owns a car showroom. At the moment she has a special offer but only for cars in her show room that cost £20,000 or more. If the customer has the special discount code, they can get a 5% discount off the cost of the car. However, if the car costs less than £20,000 there is no discount.

In this case a **nested if** has been used to deal with customers whose car costs more than £20,000. These customers will only get the discount when they have the special discount code. If this is not the case, they will not get the discount.

Task 5.4

Write this program using the editing window.

```python
car_cost=int(input("How much is the car?: "))
discount_code="XMAS99"
if car_cost >=20000:
    discount_code=input("What is the discount code?: ")
    if discount_code=="XMAS99":
        print("Car cost with discount is £",car_cost-(car_cost/100*5))
    else:
        print("Incorrect code. Car cost is £",car_cost)
else:
    print("Sorry your car needs to cost more than £20,000 to get a discount.")
```

Activity 5.3

1. You have been asked to write a program that converts raw student marks in an exam into 9 to 1 grades. The maximum mark is 160, if you achieve 74 or more, but less than 86 you achieve a grade 4.

Here are the grade boundaries:

Max Mark	9	8	7	6	5	4	3	2	1	U
Raw 160	134	123	112	99	86	74	52	30	9	0

Produce a program that asks for your raw exam result and then converts this result into the correct grade.

2. You work for a smart phone reseller. You have a special sale deal but only on android handsets. Customers that purchase an android handset will get a 25% discount each month for the first 6 months on a 12-month contract. The normal cost of the smart phone contract is £20 per month.

Produce a program that asks the customer if they are taking out a contract on an android handset. If they are then the program calculates the monthly cost for the first 6 months and the total cost of the 12-month contract.

6. The Use of Iteration

Quite often in programming you need to repeat an instruction or process over and over again. This is called **Iteration** and involves the use of programming constructs called **loops**. Including count and condition-controlled loops.

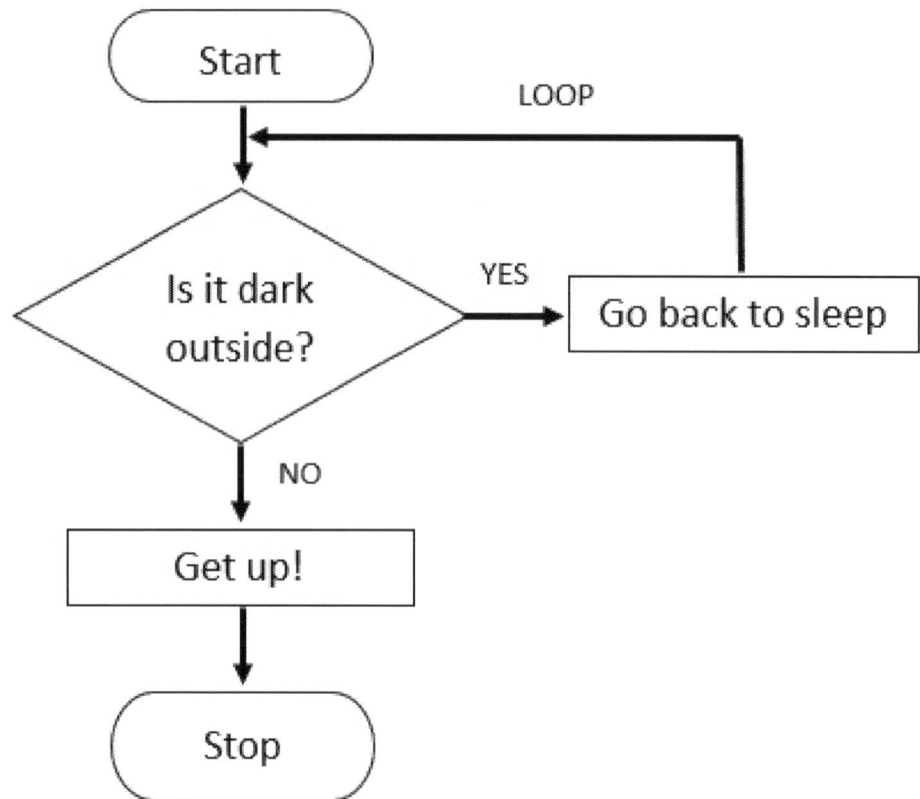

In this example the person repeatedly wakes up in the night and if it is still dark outside, they go back to sleep. They continue doing this until it is light outside and at this point, they get up.

FOR loops

For loops are examples of **definite iteration,** as when the program starts you know exactly the number of times that you are going to loop. **For loops** often use the **range** built-in function.

Top Tips
- The end of the range means up to but NOT including the final number
- Iteration also uses colons and the loops are indented in the same way that selection is indented.

Task 6.1

Write each of these example programs using the editing window and view the output.

Example 1	Example 2
In this case the value of n changes as each loop is completed. The first value for n is 0, then the program loops and the second value for n is 1. The final value is 5 as the range is up to, but not including, the final number.	In this case the beginning of the range is not included and so the program starts from 0 and the output is the same as example 1.
``
for n in range (0,6):
    print(n)
```
```
>>>
0
1
2
3
4
5
``` | ```
for n in range (6):
    print(n)
```
```
>>>
0
1
2
3
4
5
``` |

Example 3	Example 4
In this case the range is from 0 to 5 and the program repeatedly displays the text (loops through 0, 1, 2, 3 and 4).	You can also produce output that lets the numbers increase by 3 each time by adding a third number to the range.
``
for n in range (0,5):
    print("Hello World")
```
```
>>>
Hello World
Hello World
Hello World
Hello World
Hello World
``` | ```
for n in range (0,11,3):
    print(n)
```
```
>>>
0
3
6
9
>>>
``` |

FOR Loops and Strings

We can also iterate a string by using a FOR loop that repeats until the end of the string has been reached.

Task 6.2

Write this program using the editing window.

```
word1="LONDON"
for index in word1:
    print(index)
```

Here is the output produced when you run this program:

```
>>>
L
O
N
D
O
N
>>>
```

Write this program using the editing window.

```
word1="LONDON"
for index in range (0,len(word1)):
    print(word1[index])
```

Here is the output produced when you run this program:

```
L
O
N
D
O
N
```

Nested FOR Loops

We can position one loop inside another loop. In this example the first loop controls which times table will be displayed and the second loop which is nested within this loop displays the content of the table.

Task 6.3

Write this program using the editing window.

```
for index in range (2,4):
    print("This is the",index,"times table.")
    for times in range (2,13):
        print(times," x ",index," = ",index*times)
```

Here is the output produced when you run this program:

```
This is the 2 times table.
2   x   2   =   4
3   x   2   =   6
4   x   2   =   8
5   x   2   =   10
6   x   2   =   12
7   x   2   =   14
8   x   2   =   16
9   x   2   =   18
10  x   2   =   20
11  x   2   =   22
12  x   2   =   24
This is the 3 times table.
2   x   3   =   6
3   x   3   =   9
4   x   3   =   12
5   x   3   =   15
6   x   3   =   18
7   x   3   =   21
8   x   3   =   24
9   x   3   =   27
10  x   3   =   30
11  x   3   =   33
12  x   3   =   36
```

Activity 6.1

1. Use a FOR loop to display numbers from 1 to 10.

2. Use a FOR loop to display numbers from 5 to 10

3. Use a FOR loop to display numbers from 2 to 20 in steps of 2

4. Use a FOR Loop to display the word SCHOOL so that one letter from the word appears on each line.

5. Produce a program that uses only 4 lines of code that will display the 2 to 12 times table.

6. Produce a program that will display the 17 times table.

While Loops (Conditional Loops)

This type of loop iterates (repeats) until a condition is met. In the example below the condition is whether x is greater than or equal to 1. Whilst this condition is true the program will keep looping but as soon as x is equal to 1 the program will stop.

Task 6.4

Write this program using the editing window.

```
x=5
while x >=1:
    print(x)
    x=x-1
```

Here is the output produced when you run this program:

```
5
4
3
2
1
```

Watch out for an Infinite Loop!

One of the dangers of using a while loop is that the loop may continue and **never stop!** The example below is an example of a program that will generate an infinite loop as x is always going to be greater than 1.

```
x=5
while x >=1:
    print(x)
    x=x+1
```

Creating a Password Program using a WHILE loop

Task 6.5

Here is an example of a password program that uses a while loop.
Write this program using the editing window.

```
password=""
while password!="1234":
    password=input("Please enter your password: ")
    if password=="1234":
        print("Password correct. You may continue.")
    else:
        print("Incorrect password. Please try again.")
```

Here is the output produced when you run this program:

```
>>>
Please enter your password: 4321
Incorrect password. Please try again.
Please enter your password: 1234
Password correct. You may continue.
```

Using a while loop to create a menu

Using a while loop is very useful when creating a menu system. The menu will keep repeating, while the condition **carry_on** is true. When you select choice 3 (quit) then **carry_on** becomes false and the while loop stops.

Task 6.6

Write this program using the editing window and then run the program. Check that all the inputs that you enter lead to the expected outcomes.

```
question1=""
carry_on=True
while carry_on==True:
    print(" Quiz - M A I N    M E N U")
    print ("""
    1.Instructions
    2.Quiz
    3.Quit
    """)
    choice=input("What would you like to do? (Enter 1, 2 or 3):  ")
    if choice=="1":
        print("Instructions: Once you have read the question enter your answer."
    elif choice=="2":
        print("Questions")
        print("")
        question1=input("What is the capital of France?: ")
        if question1=="Paris":
            print("Correct")
    elif choice=="3":
        print("Thanks for playing. Try again soon")
        carry_on=False
    elif choice !="":
        print("Not a valid choice try again")
```

Using "Break" to leave a loop.

It is sometimes useful to use the word **Break** when the condition is met so that the block of code stops. It can be used with **FOR** and **WHILE** loops.

Task 6.7
Write each of these programs using the editing window.

```
for i in range (0,11):
    if i>=4:
        break
    print(i)
```

```
x=100
while x >10:
    if x==50:
        break
    print(x)
    x=x-10
```

Here is the output produced when you run each program:

```
>>>
0
1
2
3
```

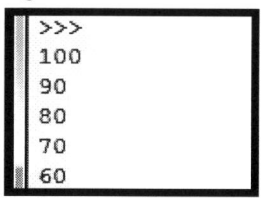

```
>>>
100
90
80
70
60
```

Activity 6.2

1. You have been asked to write a program that manages security on the personal details stored on a database. Your program must store a particular person's username and their password.

a. When this person tries to login, if their username and password are both entered correctly, they will be allowed to continue. However, if either one of these is entered incorrectly, they will be asked again to enter their username and password again. This will continue until the user name and password are entered correctly.

b. Change the program so that the person gets three chances to enter the correct username and password. After these three chances they get a message to say that they have been locked out of their account.

2 a. You have been asked to create a game. The computer stores a number and then you get a chance to guess the number. You have an unlimited number of guesses to guess the correct number. If you get the number correct you are congratulated, but every time you get the number wrong you are asked to guess again.

b. Change the game so that it is a two-player game and the players take it in turn to guess the number.

c. Create a menu system for the game. The menu system must include the rules of the game, play the game and quit.

7. The Use of Lists (Arrays)

The limitation of using variables is that they only store one item of data at any one time. An Array, which is called a **List** in python, is a data structure that can store many items of data. This data can then be viewed, manipulated and accessed.

When creating a list in Python you must use square brackets. As with **variables**, an item in a list can be the data type: string, integer, float or Boolean.

Below is a list of fruits. In this case each item has the data type **string**. An index is used to locate the position of an item in the string. Banana is at the index location 0 and Pear is at the index location 2.

Index position: 0   1   2   3   4

fruits=["Banana","Apple","Pear","Strawberry","Orange"]

Task 7.1

It is possible to select an item in a list using the index position of that item. In this case the first item is selected. Write this program using the editing window.

```
fruits=["Banana","Apple","Pear","Strawberry","Orange"]
print (fruits[0])
```

Here is the output produced when you run this program:

```
>>>
Banana
```

Task 7.2

In this case the third item is selected. Write this program using the editing window.

```
fruits=["Banana","Apple","Pear","Strawberry","Orange"]
print (fruits[2])
```

Here is the output produced when you run this program:

```
>>>
Pear
```

Slicing items in a list

It is possible to select a particular section of the list. This is called **slicing**.

Task 7.3

The example below shows a sliced list that just shows items at index 0, 1 and 2 (This means from 0 to the item before 3). Write this program using the editing window.

```
fruits=["Banana","Apple","Pear","Strawberry","Orange"]
print (fruits[0:3])
```

Here is the output produced when you run this program:

```
>>>
['Banana', 'Apple', 'Pear']
```

Task 7.4

The example below shows a sliced list that just shows items at index 2 and 3. (It stops before the last number is reached). Write this program using the editing window.

```
fruits=["Banana","Apple","Pear","Strawberry","Orange"]
print (fruits[2:4])
```

Here is the output produced when you run this program:

```
>>>
['Pear', 'Strawberry']
```

Task 7.5

The example below shows a sliced list that displays from index 2 to the end of the list. Write this program using the editing window.

```
fruits=["Banana","Apple","Pear","Strawberry","Orange"]
print (fruits[2:])
```

Here is the output produced when you run this program:

```
>>>
['Pear', 'Strawberry', 'Orange']
```

> **Activity 7.1**
>
> 1 a. Create a list (Array) of planets that are part of our solar system. The planet nearest to the Sun must be located at index 0 and as the index number increases each planet is further from the Sun.
> b. Slice the list to show the 6 planets that are nearest to the Sun.
> c. Slice the list to show the 3 planets that are furthest away from the Sun.
> d. Slice the list to show all of the planets that are further from the Sun than Earth.

Concatenate (join together) lists and sorting lists

Task 7.6

It is possible to use concatenate to join lists together. Write this program using the editing window.

```
fruits=["Banana","Apple","Pear"]
veg=["Courgette","Broccoli","Onion"]
fruitveg=fruits+veg
print(fruitveg)
```

Here is the output produced.

```
>>>
['Banana', 'Apple', 'Pear', 'Courgette', 'Broccoli', 'Onion']
>>>
```

Task 7.7

You can also concatenate lists that are made up of Integers (see below) and in this case you can also use another built-in function (**sort**) to sort the list into numerical order. Write this program using the editing window.

```
x=[5,7,11,54,61,82]
y=[3,8,13,78,91,35]
z=x+y
print(z)
z.sort()
print(z)
```

Here is the output produced

```
[5, 7, 11, 54, 61, 82, 3, 8, 13, 78, 91, 35]
[3, 5, 7, 8, 11, 13, 35, 54, 61, 78, 82, 91]
```

Activity 7.2

1 a. Create a list (Array) of planets that are part of our solar system (or use the list from activity 7.1). The planet nearest to the Sun must be located at index 0 and as the index number increases each planet is further from the Sun.

b. Now use the sort function to sort the planets into alphabetical order and then display them as a sorted list.

2. Here are two lists:
   form10a=["Jones","Ahmed","Adams","Graham"]
   form10b=["Collins","Peters","Khan","Langley"]

The forms have been merged and you have been asked to display the surnames of all of the students in the new form in alphabetical order.

3. Concatenate these two lists:
   a=[1,2,3,4,5]
   b=[6,7,8,9,10]

Adding items into a list

Sometimes when creating a program, you start with an empty or incomplete list. You can easily add to the list – This is called **appending**.

Task 7.8

Write this program using the editing window.

```
names=["Theresa", "Alana","Tayybah"]
print("List before adding",names)
names.append("Joanne")
print("List after adding",names)
```

Here is the output produced

```
List before adding ['Theresa', 'Alana', 'Tayybah']
List after adding ['Theresa', 'Alana', 'Tayybah', 'Joanne']
```

Inserting items into a list

You can also insert an item into a particular location in a list. Notice that in the example below the name has been inserted at index location 1.

Task 7.9

Write this program using the editing window.

```
names=["Theresa", "Alana","Tayybah"]
print("List before inserting",names)
names.insert(1,"Joanne")
print("List after inserting",names)
```

Here is the output produced

```
>>>
List before inserting ['Theresa', 'Alana', 'Tayybah']
List after inserting ['Theresa', 'Joanne', 'Alana', 'Tayybah']
>>>
```

How long is the list?

The method you have used to find the length of a string is similar to the method required to find the length of a list.

Task 7.10

Write this program using the editing window.

```
list1=[1,2,3,4,5,6,7,8,9,10]
list2=["Snake","Turtle","Lizard"]
print("The length of list 1 is",len(list1))
print("The length of list 2 is",len(list2))
```

Here is the output produced.

```
>>>
The length of list 1 is 10
The length of list 2 is 3
```

Is an item in the list?

Task 7.11

It is easy to check whether an item is in a list using **in**. Write this program using the editing window.

```
list2=["Snake","Turtle","Lizard"]
if "Turtle" in list2:
    print("This is in the list")
else:
    print("This is not in the list")
if "Frog" in list2:
    print("This is in the list")
else:
    print("This is not in the list")
```

Here is the output produced.

```
>>>
This is in the list
This is not in the list
```

Removing an item from a list

As well as appending items in a list you can also delete items from a list.

Task 7.12

Write this program using the editing window.

```
list2=["Snake","Turtle","Lizard"]
list2.remove("Turtle")
print(list2)
```

Here is the output produced.

```
['Snake', 'Lizard']
```

Reversing the order of a list

Task 7.13

It is sometimes useful to reverse the order of a list. Write this program using the editing window.

```
list2=["Snake","Turtle","Lizard"]
list2.reverse()
print(list2)
```

Here is the output produced.

```
>>>
['Lizard', 'Turtle', 'Snake']
```

Activity 7.3

1 You work for a UK Bank in their IT department. The bank is creating a list of customers. The bank already has these customers on their list:

  Charlotte Brown, Joe Thompson, Aisha Khan, Dipak Patel, Carla Peterson

a. Create this list in Python.

b. Add another line of code to this program that asks the customer their name.

c. Develop your program so that this name is added to the list.

d. Develop the program so that it continually asks if you have another name. If the answer is yes then the program asks the customer's name. If the answer is no then the program stops and displays the list of customers.

e. Create a menu system for your program. The menu offers the following choices:

    1. View the names on the list.

    2. Add a name to the list.

    3. Search for a name in the list.

    4. Remove a name from the list.

    5. Sort the list into alphabetical order.

    6. Quit the program

2 a. Create this list in Python:

    numbers=[1,11,56,89,54,32,54,78,90,25,56,78,43,23,23,45,65,76,78]

b. Sort the list in numerical order from low to high.

  c. Sort the list in numerical order from high to low (Reverse!)

Multiply items in a list

Task 7.14

It can be useful sometimes to multiply items in a list. Write this program using the editing window.

```
numbers=[1,2,3,4,5]
fruit=["Banana","Apple"]
print(numbers*2)
print(numbers*3)
print(fruit*2)
```

Here is the output produced.

```
[1, 2, 3, 4, 5, 1, 2, 3, 4, 5]
[1, 2, 3, 4, 5, 1, 2, 3, 4, 5, 1, 2, 3, 4, 5]
['Banana', 'Apple', 'Banana', 'Apple']
>>>
```

Two dimensional arrays (Lists)

So far, we have looked at simple lists. These are called **one dimensional arrays**. Usually the information we need to store is more complex. In this case we need to use **two dimensional arrays** (2D Lists). These are sometimes called lists of lists.

Here is an example of a two-dimensional list that stores names and ages:

```
name_age=[["Joe",22],["Celia",35],["Jane",45]]
```

It is important to know the location of an item in a list using the index.

For example, Joe is at 0, 0 and Jane's age is at 2, 1

Index position within outer list	0		1		2	
Index position within inner list	0	1	0	1	0	1
Item	Joe	22	Celia	35	Jane	45

Selecting an item in a 2D list

Task 7.15

You can use the **index position** to locate an item in a 2D list. Write this program using the editing window.

```
name_age=[["Joe",22],["Celia",35],["Jane",45]]
print(name_age[0][0])
print(name_age[2][1])
```

Here is the output produced.

```
Joe
45
```

Here is another example.

Index position within outer list	0				1				2			
Index position within inner list	0	1	2	3	0	1	2	3	0	1	2	3
Item	Helen	78	68	48	Harry	57	37	46	Toni	89	67	56

Task 7.16

In this case we are using the index location to access Helen's last test result (0, 3) and Toni's last test result (2, 3). Write this program using the editing window.

```
results=[["Helen",78,68,48],["Harry",57,37,46],["Toni",89,67,56]]
print(results[0][3])
print(results[2][3])
```

Here is the output produced.

```
48
56
>>>
```

Adding a list to an existing 2D list using append.

Sometimes you need to be able to add a list to a 2D list.

Task 7.17

For example, I have the results of another student called Chantelle who got 78, 47 and 67 in her tests. I wish to add her results to the existing list. Write this program using the editing window.

```
results=[["Helen",78,68,48],["Harry",57,37,46],["Toni",89,67,56]]
newentry=[]
name=input("What is your name?: ")
test1=input("Enter test 1 result: ")
test2=input("Enter test 2 result: ")
test3=input("Enter test 3 result: ")
newentry.append(name)
newentry.append(test1)
newentry.append(test2)
newentry.append(test3)
results.append(newentry)
print(results)
```

Here is the output produced.

```
What is your name?: Chantelle
Enter test 1 result: 78
Enter test 2 result: 47
Enter test 3 result: 67
[['Helen', 78, 68, 48], ['Harry', 57, 37, 46], ['Toni', 89, 67, 56]
, ['Chantelle', '78', '47', '67']]
```

Adding a single item to each list.

Sometimes you want to be able to add an individual item to each list. This can be done using a **FOR** loop that asks the result for each person in the list.

Task 7.18

Write this program using the editing window.

```
results=[["Helen",78,68,48],["Harry",57,37,46],["Toni",89,67,56]]
for i in range (0,len(results)):
    name=results[i][0]
    print(name)
    test4=input("Test result: ")
    results[i].insert(4,test4)
print(results)
```

Here is the output produced.

```
>>>
Helen
Test result: 67
Harry
Test result: 45
Toni
Test result: 67
[['Helen', 78, 68, 48, '67'], ['Harry', 57, 37, 46, '45'],
['Toni', 89, 67, 56, '67']]
```

Searching a 2D list

Task 7.19

It is also possible to search for an item or group of items in a 2D List. The program below looks though the list of lists and if it finds a match it will then display the information for that particular person. Write this program using the editing window.

```
results=[["Helen",78,68,48],["Harry",57,37,46],["Toni",89,67,56]]
name=input("Searching for name: ")
for i in results:
    if name in i:
        print("Found")
        print(i)
```

Here is the output produced.

```
>>>
Searching for name: Harry
Found
['Harry', 57, 37, 46]
```

Displaying a 2D list as a table

Task 7.20

Once you have created a 2D list you may wish to display the list in the form of a table. You can use formatting to make sure the list is organised into a table. Write this program using the editing window.

```
results=[["Name","Test 1","Test 2","Test 3"],["Helen",78,68,48],["Harry",57,37,46],["Toni",89,67,56]]
for a,b,c,d in results:
    print("{0:15}{1:<15}{2:<15}{3:<15}".format(a,b,c,d))
```

Here is the output produced.

```
>>>
Name           Test 1         Test 2         Test 3
Helen          78             68             48
Harry          57             37             46
Toni           89             67             56
```

Activity 7.4

1 a. Create a 2D list (Array) of the five planets in our solar system that are nearest to the Sun. Include the distance of each planet from the Sun (in millions of Kilometres) and the number of moons each one has. The planet nearest to the Sun must be located at index 0 and as the index number increases each planet is further from the Sun.

b. Develop a program that can search for planet Earth and then display the planets distance from the Sun and its number of moons.

c. A new planet called "Alderaan" has been discovered at 100 million km from the Sun. It has 1 moon. Add this to your 2D array.

d. Now add to the 2D array how long it takes for each planet to rotate on its axis. Alderaan rotates at the same speed as Earth.

e. Develop a program that displays all of your data in a table.

8. File Handing Operations

When creating programs, it is sometime useful to be able to store and retrieve data from an external file. If you don't export data to an external file, the data is only available whilst the program is running. Unless you say otherwise, the file is always saved to the same folder as the Python program you have produced.

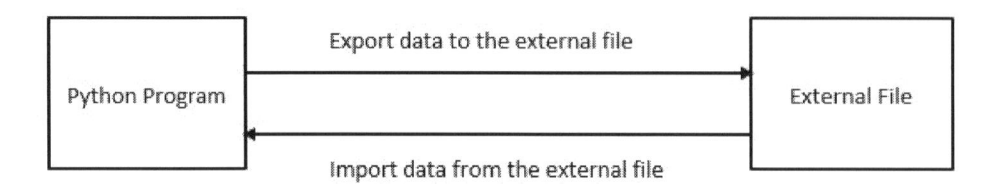

```
                    Export data to the external file
 ┌───────────────┐ ──────────────────────────────▶ ┌───────────────┐
 │ Python Program│                                  │ External File │
 └───────────────┘ ◀────────────────────────────── └───────────────┘
                    Import data from the external file
```

Modes for Reading and Writing Files

Different modes are used according to what you want the program to do.

Mode	Meaning
r	Read mode used when the file is being read into the program
w	Write mode is used to edit and write new information to a file. Any existing file with the same name will have their information deleted and replaced with the new information.
a	Append mode is used to add (append) new information to an existing file.
r+	This is a special mode used to allow both read and write actions to be performed.

How do I write information to a file?

You have a line of text that you would like to send to an external file. In this case the sentence is exported an external file called **Star Wars.txt**. The mode used is **w** as we are writing the sentence to the file. You must use close at the end to make sure the file is closed.

When you run the program nothing appears to happen, but if you look in the same folder as the Python program you will find a text file called **Star Wars** and if you open this file you will find the sentence.

Write to an external file

Task 8.1

Write this program using the editing window.

```
#Send information to an external file
sentence="May the force be with you"
file=open("Star Wars.txt","w")
file.write(sentence)
file.close()
```

This program will output the sentence to the external file.

Write to an external file and automatically close the file

Task 8.2

Sometimes you want to write a program that automatically closes the file. Write this program using the editing window.

```
sentence="May the force be with you"
with open("Star Wars.txt","w") as file:
    file.write(sentence)
```

This program will output the sentence to the external file.

How do I write a list to an external file?

You can also write a list (array) to an external file. In this case it is a good idea to write the file as a csv file as the table can then be viewed within a spreadsheet. To do this you must import the csv module.

Task 8.3

The program below will take the list and export it to a csv file which can then be viewed from within a spreadsheet. This will appear in the same folder as the Python program. Write this program using the editing window.

```python
import csv
results=[["Name","Test 1","Test 2","Test 3"],["Helen",78,68,48],["Harry",57,37,46],["Toni",89,67,56]]
with open("Test Table.csv","w",newline="") as file:
    writer=csv.writer(file)
    for n in results:
        writer.writerow(n)
```

Here is the output produced in the external file.

	A	B	C	D	E
1	Name	Test 1	Test 2	Test 3	
2	Helen	78	68	48	
3	Harry	57	37	46	
4	Toni	89	67	56	

How do I read information from a file back into my program?

If you have already created a text file it is possible to read the text from this file back into your program.

Task 8.4

In the example shown below a notepad file has been created containing the text Hello World. This has then been saved as Hello.txt. The program below has been written to take the text from the external file and assign it to the variable **text**. Write this program using the editing window.

```python
with open ("Hello.txt","r") as file:
    text=file.read()
print(text)
```

Here is the output produced.

```
>>>
Hello World
```

How do I read a list from a file back into my program?

If you have created the list using a csv file then by performing the reverse of the operation shown earlier it is possible to read the csv file back into an empty list.

Task 8.5

Write this program using the editing window.

```
import csv
results=[]
with open("Test Table.csv","r") as file:
    reader=csv.reader(file)
    results=list(reader)
print(results)
```

Here is the output produced.

```
>>>
[['Name', 'Test 1', 'Test 2', 'Test 3'], ['Helen', '78', '68', '48']
, ['Harry', '57', '37', '46'], ['Toni', '89', '67', '56']]
```

Activity 8.1
1. Here are the instructions for a game.
First player 1 must throw the dice. If the player throws a 6 they have won the game. If not then player 2 throws the dice. This continues until one of the players throws a 6 and wins the game.
(a) Develop a program that writes the instructions shown above to an external file called Instructions.txt
(b) Develop the program so that the contents of the external file can be read back into the program and stored using a variable called instructions.
2. (a) You have been asked to create a program using Python that asks the user their name, their favourite band, their favourite singer and their favourite song. The program stores this information in a list and exports the information to an external file.
(b) You have been asked to create another program that can take the information stored in the external file produced in part a, and then import it back into a list. The program then displays the list as a formatted table.

9. Using Functions and Procedures

Python programmers often have to write large complex programs. To make this manageable these programs are divided into smaller programs that perform a particular task. These are called sub-routines. There are two types of sub-routine - procedures and functions.

Functions- These are called by the main program and then return a value to the main program.

Procedures - These are called by the main program, carried out and then the main program continues.

In Python both functions and procedures are written in the same way. **Def** is used to define the function/procedure.

Task 9.1

Here is an example of a function. Write this program using the editing window.

```
def add_numbers(x, y):
    result = x+y
    print(result)
```

To make the function do something you must **call** it. Here is the output produced if x is 3 and y is 5.

```
>>> add_numbers(3,5)
8
>>>
```

The function is being called.

Task 9.2

Here is an example of a procedure. Write this program using the editing window.
What does the procedure do? Call the procedure to find out.

```
def count(x):
    for x in range(1,1000):
        x=x+1
```

Built in Functions in Python

Python includes some functions (sub-routines) that are ready for you to use. For example, **print()** is a built-in function and so is **input()**. You can do a search online to get a full list of built-in functions.

Use of Modules

A module is a bit like a group of functions used to perform a particular task.

For example, a commonly used module is the random module. This can be used to select a random number. If you want to use a module you must import it before you use it.

Task 9.3

Here is an example of the **random** module. Write this program using the editing window.

```
import random
print("Throw the dice.........")
dice_throw=random.randint(1,6)
print("You got a: ",dice_throw)
```

Here is the output produced.

```
Throw the dice.........
You got a:  5
```

Arguments and Parameters

Values produced by a function can be **returned** to the main program when it is called.
and values produced by the main program can also be passed to the function. Values passed from the main program to the function are called **arguments**. The name given to the "holder" of the argument is called the **parameter**.

    add_numbers(x,y):

        z=x+y

        return z

In this case **x** and **y** are **parameters**. If the function is "called" then the values entered are called the arguments. In this case 2 and 3 are the arguments.

    add_numbers(2,3)

Task 9.4

In this example x and y are the parameters and the arguments are Fred and Bloggs. Write this program using the editing window.

```
def info(x,y):
    print("Details: ",x,y)
first_name=input("First name:")
surname=input("Surname: ")
info(first_name,surname)
```

Here is the output produced.

```
First name:Fred
Surname: Bloggs
Details:   Fred Bloggs
```

Task 9.5

In the program below the value produced by the function is returned to the main program. Write this program using the editing window and then run the program.

```
def change(cost,payment):
    change=payment-cost
    return change
item_cost=float(input("Please enter the cost of the item: "))
payment_made=float(input("Please enter customer payment: "))
change_needed=change(item_cost,payment_made)
print("Change given: ",change_needed)
```

Local and Global Variables

If the variable is only available within the function/procedure it is called a local variable
If the variable is available anywhere within the programme it is called a global variable.

This difference is important as when you only use a variable within a function/procedure it will not be known to the main program. If you do want to use a variable from inside a function/procedure in the main program then you will need to declare it as a global variable.

Task 9.6

In the program below the variable x is used inside the variable and in the main program. Write this program using the editing window and then run the program. Delete the line **global x** and run the program again – What happens? Why is this?

```
def test():
    global x
    x = "Hello World"
    print(x)
test()
print(x)
```

Activity 9.1
1. Here are the instructions for a game: **First player 1 must throw the dice. If the player throws a 6 they have won the game. If not then player 2 throws the dice. This continues until one of the players throws a 6 and wins the game.** (a) Write a function that writes the instructions shown above to an external file called Instructions.txt (b) Write a function that reads the content of the external file back into the program and stores this information using a variable called instructions. 2. (a) You have been asked to create a program using Python that asks the user their name, their favourite band, their favourite singer and their favourite song. The program stores this information in a list and exports the information to an external file. Write this program using a function. (b) You have been asked to create another program that can take the information stored in the external file produced in part a, and then import it back into a list. The program then displays the list as a formatted table. Write this program using a function.

10. Creating a Board Game

Getting started

A simple way to create a game board is using a list with every number from the game board. If you want a board like the one below you will need 4 numbers.

4	3
1	2

Task 10.1

Remember the positions in a list start from 0, and so number 1 in the list is found in the position 0 and number two in the position 1. Write this program using the editing window.

```
board=[1,2,3,4]
print(board[3],board[2])
print(board[0],board[1])
```

Here is the output produced.

```
4 3
1 2
```

Task 10.2

You can use print statements to make it more like a game board.
Add this to your Python code. Write this program using the editing window.

```
board=[1,2,3,4]
print(".......")
print(board[3],":",board[2])
print(".......")
print(board[0],":",board[1])
print(".......")
```

Here is the output produced.

```
. . . . . .
4  :  3
. . . . . .
1  :  2
. . . . . .
```

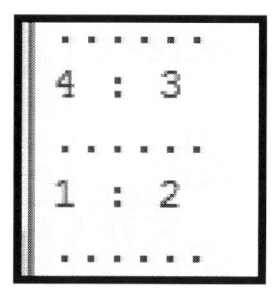

Task 10.3

If you want to create a bigger board, then it is easier if you use a **FOR** loop to add the numbers to the list. Write this program using the editing window.

```
board=[]
for n in range (1,26):
    board.append(n)

print(board[20],":",board[21],":",board[22],":",board[23],":",board[24])
print("......................")
print(board[19],":",board[18],":",board[17],":",board[16],":",board[15])
print("......................")
print(board[10],":",board[11],":",board[12],":",board[13],":",board[14])
print("......................")
print(board[9],":",board[8]," :",board[7]," :",board[6]," :",board[5])
print("......................")
print(board[0]," :",board[1]," :",board[2]," :",board[3]," :",board[4])
```

Here is the output produced.

```
21 : 22 : 23 : 24 : 25
. . . . . . . . . . . . . . . . . . . . . .
20 : 19 : 18 : 17 : 16
. . . . . . . . . . . . . . . . . . . . . .
11 : 12 : 13 : 14 : 15
. . . . . . . . . . . . . . . . . . . . . .
10 :  9 :  8 :  7 :  6
. . . . . . . . . . . . . . . . . . . . . .
1  :  2 :  3 :  4 :  5
>>>
```

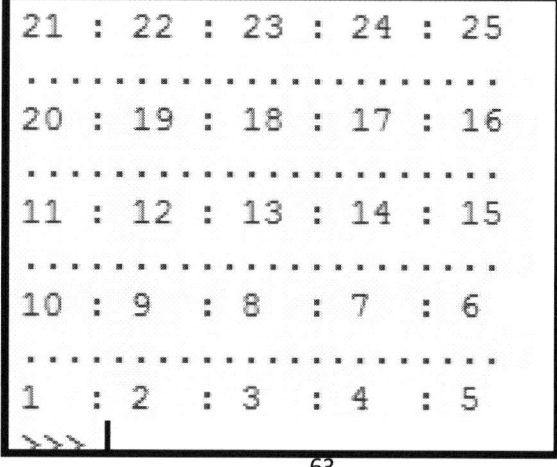

Activity 10.1

Clark is designing a game that allows players to move around a 7x7 grid, each position in the board has a number to represent the space, as shown in Fig 1.

Create this game board.

43	44	45	46	47	48	49
42	41	40	39	38	37	36
29	30	31	32	33	34	35
28	27	26	25	24	23	22
15	16	17	18	19	20	21
14	13	12	11	10	9	8
1	2	3	4	5	6	7

Fig 1

Creating a game board function

When writing code for a whole game it's a good idea to decompose the game into sub-tasks. One of these sub-tasks could be making the game board into a function that can be repeatedly used.

Task 10.4

Edit the Python code you have already used to turn the board into a function.

```
board=[]
for n in range(1,26):
    board.append(n)

def displayboard():
    print("")
    print(board[20],":",board[21],":",board[22],":",board[23],":",board[24])
    print("."*23)
    print(board[19],":",board[18],":",board[17],":",board[16],":",board[15])
    print("."*23)
    print(board[10],":",board[11],":",board[12],":",board[13],":",board[14])
    print("."*23)
    print(board[9],":",board[8]," :",board[7]," :",board[6]," :",board[5])
    print("."*23)
    print(board[0]," :",board[1]," :",board[2]," :",board[3]," :",board[4])
    print("")
```

When you run the code nothing happens, because for a function to work you need to call it. Add an extra line of code to call the function (see below).

```
board=[]
for n in range(1,26):
    board.append(n)

def displayboard():
    print("")
    print(board[20],":",board[21],":",board[22],":",board[23],":",board[24])
    print("."*23)
    print(board[19],":",board[18],":",board[17],":",board[16],":",board[15])
    print("."*23)
    print(board[10],":",board[11],":",board[12],":",board[13],":",board[14])
    print("."*23)
    print(board[9],":",board[8]," :",board[7]," :",board[6]," :",board[5])
    print("."*23)
    print(board[0]," :",board[1]," :",board[2]," :",board[3]," :",board[4])
    print("")

displayboard()
```

Here is the output produced.

```
21 : 22 : 23 : 24 : 25
.......................
20 : 19 : 18 : 17 : 16
.......................
11 : 12 : 13 : 14 : 15
.......................
10 : 9  : 8  : 7  : 6
.......................
1  : 2  : 3  : 4  : 5
```

How to roll a dice

Task 10.5

To roll a dice you must import the **random module**. Write this program using the editing window.

```
#Simple dice throw
import random
dice1=int(0)
play=input("Do you want to roll the dice?")
if play=="Y":
    dice1=random.randint(1,6)
    print("You got a: ",dice1)
```

> **Activity 10.2**
>
> Create a program that enables a player to throw **two** dice. The program then tells the player their score from each dice. The program then tells the player the total score (the score when the dice throws are added together).

Creating a two-player game

If you create a two-player game then you need each player to take it in turn to throw the dice.

Task 10.6

The code below is for the first player. Write this program using the editing window and then write the code for the **second player**.

```
import random
board = []
totalp1=0
totalp2=0
turn=1
no_win=True

def displayboard(board):
    print("")
    print(board[20],":",board[21],":",board[22],":",board[23],":",board[24])
    print("."*23)
    print(board[19],":",board[18],":",board[17],":",board[16],":",board[15])
    print("."*23)
    print(board[10],":",board[11],":",board[12],":",board[13],":",board[14])
    print("."*23)
    print(board[9],":",board[8]," :",board[7]," :",board[6]," :",board[5])
    print("."*23)
    print(board[0]," :",board[1]," :",board[2]," :",board[3]," :",board[4])
    print("")

while no_win:
    while turn ==1:
        board=[]
        print("Player 1 it's your turn.")
        throw = input("Press R to roll the dice: ")
        if throw == "R":
            for n in range(1,26):
                board.append(n)
            dice=random.randint(1,6)
            print("Player 1 - You have thrown a: ",dice)
            totalp1=totalp1+dice
            board[totalp1]="P1"
            displayboard(board)
            turn=2
```

Task 10.7

When you create this two-player game there are some limitations.
- The board only displays the player (e.g. P1) on the game board when it is the players turn.
- The game does not take into account what would happen if two players landed on the same spot on the board.

To overcome these problems the code will need to be adjusted. To overcome the first limitation, you will need to add a line of code to the program for each player.

```
board[totalp2]="P2"
board[totalp1]="P1"
```

This means that both players will be displayed on the board at the same time.

Task 10.8

The second limitation is a little more complicated to resolve. The total score for each player would have to be identical and then you would need to display P1P2 in the same square.

Adapt you code for player 1 and 2 so that it is as shown below.

```
while no_win:
    while turn ==1 and no_win:
        board=[]
        print("Player 1 it's your turn.")
        throw = input("Press R to roll the dice: ")
        if throw == 'R':
            for n in range(1,26):
                board.append(n)
            dice=random.randint(1,6)
            print("Player 1 - You have thrown a: ",dice)
            totalp1=totalp1+dice
            if totalp1==totalp2:
                board[totalp1]="P1P2"
                displayboard(board)
                turn=1
            else:
                board[totalp1]="P1"
                board[totalp2]="P2"
                print("Player 1 - Your total score is: ",totalp1)
                displayboard(board)
                turn=2
    while turn ==2 and no_win:
        board=[]
        print("Player 2 it's your turn.")
        throw = input("Press R to roll the dice: ")
        if throw == 'R':
            for n in range(1,26):
                board.append(n)
            dice=random.randint(1,6)
            print("Player 2 - You have thrown a: ",dice)
            totalp2=totalp2+dice
            if totalp1==totalp2:
                board[totalp2]="P1P2"
                displayboard(board)
                turn=1
            else:
                board[totalp2]="P2"
                board[totalp1]="P1"
                print("Player 2 - Your total score is: ",totalp2)
                displayboard(board)
                turn=1
```

Winning the game

The first player who gets to the final number on the board wins the game. As the game goes on you are keeping a record of the total score for each player. If there are 25 numbers on the grid then it is the first player to reach or exceed 25 on the board.

Task 10.9

Adapt your code to show the winner of the game. Here is the code for player 1.

```
while no_win:
    while turn ==1 and no_win:
        board=[]
        print("Player 1 it's your turn.")
        throw = input("Press R to roll the dice: ")
        if throw == 'R':
            for n in range(1,26):
                board.append(n)
            dice=random.randint(1,6)
            print("Player 1 - You have thrown a: ",dice)
            totalp1=totalp1+dice
            if totalp1>=25:
                    print("Player 1 - You are the winner!")
                    no_win=False
                    break
            if totalp1==totalp2:
                board[totalp1]="P1P2"
                displayboard(board)
                turn=1
            else:
                board[totalp1]="P1"
                board[totalp2]="P2"

                print("Player 1 - Your total score is: ",totalp1)
                displayboard(board)
                turn=2
```

Importing a message that is stored externally.

Task 10.10

Create a notepad file called **rules** and enter the rules of the game in this file (This notepad file must be in the same folder as your Python program).
Add this code to your game and then run the program:

```python
def read_file():
    with open ("rules.txt","r") as file:
        text=file.read()
        print(text)
read_file()
```

The output from this part of the program is:

```
>>>
Game Rules - You must take it in turns to throw a dice.The first player to get to the last number on the game board is the winner.
```

Adding obstacles to a game

Games like this e.g. Snakes and Ladders, often have obstacles. If you land on an obstacle you move backwards a certain number of spaces.

To do this you will need to create a variable that stores information about where the obstacle is on the board.

Task 10.11

Start by adding the variable and assigning it a value. Add this code to your game and then run the program:

```python
import random
board = []
play="Y"
totalp1=0
totalp2=0
no_win=True
turn=1
obstacle=12
```

Task 10.12

Now edit the code for player 1 (you will need to repeat this for player 2).

```
while no_win:
    while turn ==1 and no_win:
        board=[]
        print("Player 1 it's your turn.")
        throw = input("Press R to roll the dice: ")
        if throw == 'R':
            for n in range(1,26):
                board.append(n)
            dice=random.randint(6,6)
            print("Player 1 - You have thrown a: ",dice)
            totalp1=totalp1+dice
            if totalp1==obstacle:
                totalp1=2
                print("You have landed on an obstacle - Go back 10 spaces")
            if totalp1>=25:
                print("Player 1 - You are the winner!")
                no_win=False
                break
            if totalp1==totalp2:
                board[totalp1]="P1P2"
                displayboard(board)
                turn=1
            else:
                board[totalp1]="P1"
                board[totalp2]="P2"

                print("Player 1 - Your total score is: ",totalp1)
                displayboard(board)
                turn=2
```

Activity 10.3

Helen is designing a computer board game called "Quiz Board". The game is played on a 10 x 10 grid with the first position on the grid starting at 1 and the last position ending at 100 (see figure 1).

100	99	98	97	96	95	94	93	92	91
81	82	83	84	85	86	87	88	89	90
80	79	78	77	76	75	74	73	72	71
61	62	63	64	65	66	67	68	69	70
60	59	58	57	56	55	54	53	52	51
41	42	43	44	45	46	47	48	49	50
40	39	38	37	36	35	34	33	32	31
21	22	23	24	25	26	27	28	29	30
20	19	18	17	16	15	14	13	12	11
1	2	3	4	5	6	7	8	9	10

Figure 1

The game is played by two players who take it in turn to throw three 6-sided dice. Both players start at position 1 on the board. If player 1 throws a three, a four and a five, they will move 12 spaces to position 12 on the board.

The winner is the first player to get to space 100 although players do not need to land exactly on space 100, for example if they are on 95 and they roll a seven, they will still win the game.

Analyse the requirements for this system and design, develop, test and evaluate a program that:

1. Asks each player their name before the game starts.
2. Allows both named players to take it in turns to play the game.
3. Each player takes it in turn to throw three dice.
4. Displays the board after each turn (the board shows the player's current position).
5. Displays the messages below:
    a. Instructions message: You must write a list of instructions on how to play the game.
    b. Winning message: You must write a message that tells the player that they have won the game.

    These messages should be stored externally and then read into the game at the start of the program.

6. At the beginning of the game 5 quiz question positions are generated. If the player lands on one of these quiz positions they get asked a random quiz question (from a bank of 5 questions). If they get the answer correct, they move an extra 10 spaces forward. However, if they get the question wrong, they move back 10 spaces.

11. Creating a Database using Python Lists

Database Login

Databases often store personal and sensitive information and so a secure login is essential to authenticate that the user has permission to access the database.

Task 11.1

The database used in this example is a database of Music Artists.

The person who wishes to use the database has the username: **tswift** and the password: **1234** (This password is not recommended, but can be used whilst testing the database).

Copy this code into Python:

```python
print("*"*50)
print("Music Database")
print("*"*50)
username="tswift"
password="1234"

username=input("Enter your username: ")
password=input("Enter your password: ")

while username!="tswift" or password!="1234":
    print("Username or password incorrect")
    print("Please try again")
    username=input("Enter your username: ")
    password=input("Enter your password: ")

else:
    print("Welcome to the Music Database")
```

Activity 11.1

1. (a) Copy the table below and complete it:

Test	Expected Result	Actual Result
A correct username but an incorrect password		
An incorrect username but a correct password		
A correct password and username		
An incorrect password and an incorrect username		

(b) Why is it important to carry out these tests?

Database Menu

When you create a database, you need to have a menu system to be able to select different aspects of the database. We need a menu that lets you add a new song to the database and search for a particular song.

Task 11.2

Add this code to the Python program you have started:

```python
selection=True
while selection:
    print("*"*50)
    print("Music Database")
    print("""
    1. Add a new song
    2. Search for a song
    3. Report - View all songs on the database
    4. Logout
    """)
    selection=input("Please select 1-4 from the options shown above: ")
    if selection=="1":
        print("So you want to add a new song.")
    elif selection=="2":
        print("So you want to search the database.")
    elif selection=="3":
        print("So you want to view a list of all songs on the database.")
    elif selection=="4":
        print("Thank you for using the Music Database")
        break
    elif selection!="":
        print("Not a valid selection")
```

Activity 11.2
Add another suitable choice to the menu and run the program to test whether this choice can be selected.

Adding a Record to the Database

To add a record to the database you must check whether the song is already on the database and then get the user to input the information about a song. Once you have gathered the information you can then transfer it to the external data file.

Task 11.3

Create a Notepad file called **music database** and save it in the save folder as your Python file.
Add this code to the top of the Python program you have started (you need to declare these variables and the list):

```
song_name=()
genre=()
year=()
name_artist=()
findsong=()
list=[]
```

Task 11.4

Add this code to the Python program for menu choice 1:

```python
if selection=="1":
    #This code enables the user to add a new song
    print("So you want to add a new song.")
    song_name=input("Enter the name of your song: ")

    #This line checks if the song is already on the database
    while song_name in open("music_database.txt").read():
        print("This song is already on the database")
        song_name=input("Enter a song that is not on the database: ")

    #The data is added to the list
    list.append(song_name)
    name_artist=input("Enter the name of the artist: ")
    list.append(name_artist)
    year=input("Enter the year the song was released: ")
    list.append(year)
    genre=input("Enter the genre: ")
    list.append(genre)
    print("You have entered the following details: ",list)

    #This code transfers the data to a file called music_database
    liststr = [str(element) for element in list]
    record=" ".join(liststr)
    print("The following song has been added to the database")
    print(record)
    songfile=open("music_database.txt","a+")
    songfile.write(record)
    songfile.write("\n")
    songfile.close()
    list = []
```

Searching the Database for a Particular Record

A database is only useful if you can search for the information you are looking for.

Task 11.5

Add this code to the Python program for menu choice 2:

```python
elif selection=="2":
    file = open("music_database.txt", "r+")
    print("So you want to search the database for a particular song.")
    find_song=input("Enter the name of the song you are searching for: ")
    for line in file:
        if find_song in line:
            print("Song found: ")
            print(line)
```

Display the Database

It is sometimes useful to display the records in a database.

Task 11.6

Add this code to the Python program for menu choice 3:

```
elif selection=="3":
    print("So you want to view a list of all songs on the database.")
    file = open("music_database.txt","r+")
    print("Here is a complete list of all songs on the database: ")
    for line in file:
        print(line)
    file.close()
```

Activity 11.3

1. Add a new menu item that lets the user choose a music genre and then all of the records of that genre are displayed. For example, the user chooses the genre "pop" and then all of the "pop" songs on the database are displayed.
2. Complete the code for the final menu item to allow the user to quit the database

Activity 11.4

Rob works in the admin department at Archside Academy. He has been asked by the headteacher to create a secure database system to manage detentions within the school. When a detention is set a unique number is used to identify it.

Rob wants to be able to have a user-friendly interface that allows him to log into the system and carry out the necessary administration.

The detention system must store the following information:

- Unique number (set by the program)
- Student name
- Form group
- Date of detention
- Time of detention
- Length of detention
- Reason for detention
- Teacher Initials

Analyse the requirements for this system and design, develop, test and evaluate a program that allows Rob to:

1. Log in with a username and password

2. Access a menu system

3. Enter and store detention information

4. Log out

5. Retrieve and display the details of any detentions by searching for a student's name.

6. Create at least two different reports that Rob might need and describe how he would use each one.

7. Produce these reports when selected from a menu.

Printed in Poland
by Amazon Fulfillment
Poland Sp. z o.o., Wrocław